Meet Our New Student From

ZAMBIA

John A. Torres

PUBLISHERS
P.O. Box 196
Hockessin, Delaware 19707
Visit us on the web: www.mitchelllane.com
Comments? email us: mitchelllane@mitchelllane.com

Mitchell Lane
PUBLISHERS

Meet Our New Student From

Australia • China • Colombia • Great Britain
• Haiti • India • Israel • Japan • Korea • Malaysia •
Mali • Mexico • New Zealand • Nicaragua • Nigeria
• Quebec • South Africa • Tanzania • Zambia •
Going to School Around the World

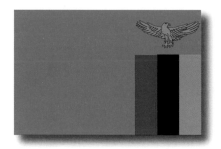

Copyright © 2010 by Mitchell Lane Publishers

All rights reserved. No part of this book
may be reproduced without written permission
from the publisher. Printed and bound in the
United States of America.

PUBLISHER'S NOTE: The facts on which the story
in this book is based have been thoroughly
researched. Documentation of such research
can be found on page 44. While every possible
effort has been made to ensure accuracy, the
publisher will not assume liability for damages
caused by inaccuracies in the data, and
makes no warranty on the accuracy of the
information contained herein.

**Library of Congress
Cataloging-in-Publication Data applied for.**

Printing   1   2   3   4   5   6   7   8   9

PLB

CONTENTS

Chapter One
Mr. Sagarin Makes an Announcement 5

Chapter Two
A Brief History of Zambia 13

Chapter Three
The Land 19

Chapter Four
Culture and Customs 25

Chapter Five
Mulishani, Franco! 35

Zambian Recipe: *Nshima* **with Pineapple Chutney** 41

Craft: How to Make a Tonga Basket 42

Further Reading 44

    Books 44

    Works Consulted 44

    On the Internet 44

    Embassy 45

Glossary 46

Index 47

Zambia

In the capital city of Lusaka, much of the shopping occurs in open-air markets where street vendors sell their wares.

Mr. Sagarin Makes an
Announcement

Chapter

It was a sleepy Monday morning—sleepier than usual. It was the first day back after spring break, and everyone in my fourth-grade class—including me—was yawning like crazy.

Even though I like school a lot, and I really like my teacher, Mr. Sagarin—he lets us call him Fred—I was wishing I still had one day of vacation left. But here we were, getting ready for class at Eleanor Roosevelt Elementary School in the small town where I live in the Hudson Valley area of New York.

The snow had finally melted, and the warming spring air seemed to make everyone even sleepier. But I was sure Mr. Sagarin would liven things up real soon. He lives on a farm and is always bringing in cool things to share, like snakes or frogs or some type of vegetable that he grew. One time he even brought his horse.

But nothing could prepare any of us for how Mr. Sagarin looked that morning. He walked in slowly,

FACTS ABOUT REPUBLIC OF ZAMBIA

Total Area:
290,586 square miles
(752,618 square kilometers)

Population:
11,862,740 (July 2009 estimate)

Capital City: Lusaka

Monetary Unit: Zambian kwacha (ZMK)

Ethnic Groups: Africans (includes Bemba, Tonga, Chewa, Lozi, Nsenga, Tumbuka, Ngoni, Lala, Kaonde, Lunda, and others

Religions: Christianity, Islam, and Hinduism, with some people practicing indigenous beliefs

Official Languages: Bemba (official), Nyanja (official), Tonga (official), Lozi (official), Chewa, Nsenga, Tumbuka. Lunda (official), Kaonde (official), Lala, Luvale (official), English (official)

Chief Exports: Copper, cobalt, electricity, tobacco, flowers, cotton

wearing a colorful wrap on his head and a long flowing red, blue, and yellow dress over his clothes. And he was balancing a jug of water on his head.

At first everyone was laughing, but then we quieted down and watched, worried that he might spill the water.

We all sighed when he finally made it to his desk and put down the jug. Then we stared as he removed the dress and then the wrap from his head. We didn't know why he wore those things or what they were, but we knew they weren't from his farm.

Mr. Sagarin pulled down a large colorful map of the world. "Class," he said, "I have a very exciting announcement to make. Tomorrow, we will have a new student in our class from a country very far away."

"Where, Fred?" I blurted out, without raising my hand. I was suddenly wide awake. It's not often you get to meet someone who was born in another country.

"Well, Mr. Danny Parker, even though you called out without raising your hand, I'll

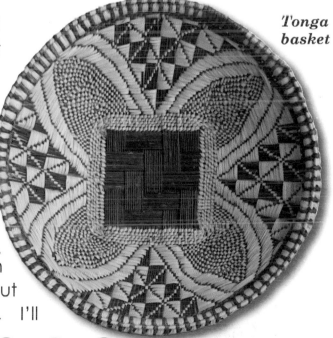

Tonga basket

Girls pump water at a local well. They will fill several jugs and carry the water back to their homes. Not many areas of Zambia have indoor plumbing.

answer the question." Mr. Sagarin took his laser pointer and moved it from New York very slowly to the right, then went lower and lower until he reached the continent of Africa. There, he moved it over Liberia, Nigeria, and Egypt, and then even lower. Finally he settled the pointer on a small country next to Angola.

"Here," he said. "Franco is from the country of Zambia." He pronounced it ZAM-bee-ya.

"Zambia?" I asked. "Where exactly is that?" But before I could finish my sentence, other kids began calling out questions of their own.

"Is Franco a boy or a girl?"

"Does he wear a dress like the one you're wearing?

"What do they eat there?"

"Do they play baseball?"

Mr. Sagarin raised his hands and calmed everyone down. He told us our questions were very good, and that most of them would probably be answered in a few moments when he told us a little bit about Franco.

"First, Franco is a ten-year-old boy," he explained. "He loves to play soccer, tag, and checkers. The colorful clothes I wore today are typical of what Zambian girls wear."

By the end of the day, Mr. Sagarin filled us in on some of the details of Franco's life. We learned that Franco spoke a little English, but that his main language was a dialect of Zulu. He told us Zambia is in sub-Saharan Africa. We learned that Zambia used to be a British colony—which is why some people there speak English.

But then we learned that Zambia is one of the countries in Africa where a terrible disease called **AIDS** has killed a lot of people. Franco's parents

A girl washes clothes in a metal tub as she cares for a younger sibling. Many children carry younger brothers and sisters on their backs.

Children enjoy seeing images of themselves on a digital camera. Many of the poor children in Zambia have never seen a photo of themselves.

both died of AIDS, and there are millions of children like Franco in Africa. Franco was an orphan who lived in the forest, or, as Mr. Sagarin called it, the African bush.

I felt sad for Franco, but I also could not wait to meet him.

Zambia

Family and friends thought Dr. David Livingstone was lost in the jungle or had been captured by hostile tribes. Journalist Henry Stanley set out to find him. When he did, he uttered the now famous phrase: "Dr. Livingstone, I presume."

A Brief History of
Zambia

Chapter

Zambia is a landlocked country in the southern half of Africa. It shares its borders with several other countries, including the Democratic Republic of the Congo, Tanzania, Malawi, Mozambique (moh-zam-BEEK), Zimbabwe (zim-BOB-way), Botswana, Namibia, and Angola.

The history of Zambia is not like the histories of European countries or even of the United States. Thousands of years ago, Zambia was not a country but was simply land that hunters from many different areas used. In the twelfth century, these hunters became mixed with the Tonga people, who spoke the language Bantu. This was part of what is known as the Bantu Expansion. No one really knows why the Bantu speakers expanded so quickly throughout much of Africa, but a lot of their success can be traced to their language skills.

The language was easy to learn, and using it allowed for more social situations than in the past.

Primitive (PRIH-mih-tiv) people were able to communicate better and become more advanced. They became very good farmers and metalworkers, and they learned how to raise livestock such as cattle. In modern times, many African cultures have become known for their cattle-raising skills and metalworking talents. Over the years, many other tribes and types of people came to settle in Zambia, including the Nsokolo (soh-KOH-loh) and the Ngoni (GOH-nee) peoples.

The first European to visit the area now known as Zambia was Francisco de Lacerda in 1798. Other explorers soon followed. During the eighteenth and nineteenth centuries, many African areas became the targets of European **slave traders**. These Europeans captured men, women, and children who lived in Africa, filled their large ships with these people, then sailed to other countries and sold them as slaves.

There were many people in the western world who were against the idea of slavery. One of them was **missionary** (MIH-shuh-nayr-ee) Dr. David Livingstone. He wanted to spread Christianity in China, but was soon attracted to southern Africa. A friend had told him about thousands of villages there that had never before been visited by a missionary.

During his travels—between 1852 and 1856—Livingstone ventured into the area now known as

Zambia. He was startled and amazed to see the most wondrous waterfall he could have imagined. Livingstone was the first European ever to set his eyes on Mosi-oa-Tunya, "the smoke that thunders." He gave the waterfall an English name in honor of England's queen: Victoria (vik-TOR-ee-ah) Falls.

Livingstone continued to preach against slavery. His statue stands at the falls with the words "Christianity, Commerce and Civilization." He believed these three things would be the keys to helping Africa come out from under the fist of slavery.

Unfortunately, Livingstone's exploration and works also opened the door for other Europeans, who tried to claim African lands for themselves. In 1889, a British South Africa company purchased mining rights to the copper and other precious metals found in Zambia. In the early 1900s, that area became known as Northern Rhodesia (roh-DEE-jyuh) and remained under British rule until 1964. It was named Rhodesia after Cecil Rhodes, a businessman and

CECIL JOHN
RHODES
1853-1902
YOUR HINTERLAND
IS THERE

politician who helped **colonize** (KAH-luh-nyz) South Africa.

In 1964, Britain gave up several territories under heavy political pressure, and one of the new independent nations became known as Zambia. But the people did not seem ready to start a government on their own. Very few people were educated, and when the price of copper dropped

An open copper mine in Kitwe, Zambia. Copper mining drives much of Zambia's economy.

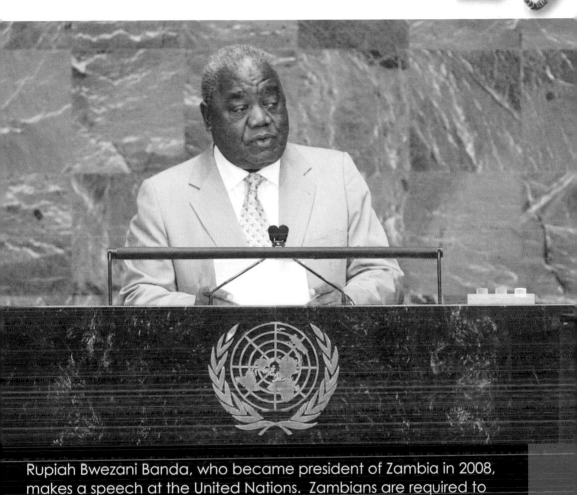

Rupiah Bwezani Banda, who became president of Zambia in 2008, makes a speech at the United Nations. Zambians are required to display a photograph of the president in their homes.

in the 1970s, Zambia began to rely more and more on international aid.

During the 1980s, the disease of AIDS crept into the country. It has continued to spread, claiming many lives and making progress in education, government, and other fields difficult.

Zambia

The breathtaking
Victoria Falls are on
the Zambezi River
between Zambia and
Zimbabwe. Mist from
the falls waters rain
forest plants at the top.

The Land

Chapter **3**

Even though the landlocked country of Zambia can boast of neither ocean view nor lush coastline, there are many beautiful sites in the sub-Saharan nation. In addition to the famous tourist site Victoria Falls, there is also the Zambezi (zam-BEE-zee) River, the Bangweulu (bong-WAY-loo) Swamps, and the Luangwa River Valley.

The country has two main river basins. The Congo basin in the north covers about 25 percent of the nation, and the much larger Zambezi basin stretches more than 3,000 miles.

The Zambezi River—one of the few rivers in the world that has sharks in it—is extremely large. Explorer Livingstone was obsessed with finding its source but never did. Impassable waters, lack of volunteers, and sickness were just a few of the obstacles that stood in his way.

Much of the wildlife in Zambia is now on game reserves, where the animals are protected. You can

Seventeen rivers drain into the basin that becomes Bangweulu Swamps, and only one drains it. The swamps evaporate after the November-to-March rainy season. Nearly 400 species of birds have been found there.

find the "Big 5" there: lions, elephants, leopards, Cape buffalo, and rhinos.

Zambia, roughly the size of Texas, consists mainly of high plateaus, mountains, and hills. Those hills keep this subtropical country cool. It is very hot for eight months of the year, but Zambia's winters—July through August—are dry but comfortable. During the winter months, the overnight temperatures can drop down to 40 degrees Fahrenheit. During the day, they are usually between 75 and 85°F.

Zambia is home to a wide variety of exotic wildlife, including the lion. Unfortunately, due to poaching and land development, much of the wildlife exists only on protected game reserves.

Zambia's year is not really separated into seasons like those in the United States. Zambia has a rainy season, a summer, and a dry season. During the rainy season, it is not uncommon to see floods that make it impossible to drive on the roads. Sometimes these floods cause treacherous mudslides.

The rainy season also breeds mosquitoes, which

*fun*FACTS

Tourists who want to see elephants, rhinos, and big cats bring much-needed money into the country.

*fun*FACTS

lay their eggs in standing water. The more rain that falls, the more mosquitoes can hatch. Mosquitoes in Zambia are more dangerous than they are in the United States, because they spread a disease known as **malaria** (muh-LAYR-ee-uh). If untreated, malaria can be deadly.

Malaria has been wiped out in most of the world's countries, but Africa is still affected by it. Many Western organizations and **charities** (CHAYR-ih-teez) are working to help rid Africa of this malady. One simple way to save lives from malaria is by providing mosquito nets to schools, hospitals, and orphanages. The insects cannot break through the nets, so those inside them are protected.

During the dry season, it does not rain for many months. The red-clay soil on the ground becomes

Health workers show people how to use a mosquito net over a bed. Simple measures like using mosquito nets can prevent people from getting malaria.

very hard. The crops dry up, and very tall grass called elephant grass grows up to six feet high. During this time of year, the winter, there can be food shortages. The people must grow and save enough food during the rainy season to last through the dry months.

Zambia

In South Luangwa, boys wearing traditional face paint perform a tribal dance as part of a performing arts program.

Culture and
Customs

Chapter

Just as roosters begin crowing right before sunrise, singing starts the day in Zambia. Despite the **poverty** and disease that have kept their country down, the people in Zambia are friendly and joyous. Many walk around singing without even realizing they are doing so. Maybe it is because they live in such a beautiful place, or maybe it is because they find joy in the religions they practice.

Zambia is made up of more than 70 different ethnic groups. This means that the culture changes from region to region throughout the small nation. For example, the capital city of Lusaka has many different ethnic groups, each with its own traditions, religions, and cultures, all living together. In more rural areas, known as the bush, ethnic groups tend to live separately in small villages.

Some villages in the bush have only a few grass huts that belong to an extended family, including aunts and uncles and grandparents. There is normally

Homes outside of Zambia's big cities are often made of clay or mud with thatched roofs. People only use their huts to sleep, spending most of their time outside.

a "chief" who is responsible for several villages. No important decisions—such as the sale of land or the opening of a business—can be made without the chief's approval. The people in the bush are **subsistence** (sub-SIS-tents) farmers. This means they grow only what they eat.

A woman tends her garden near Livingstone, Zambia. Many families have private garden plots for growing their own food.

Near Mufwe, Zambia, workers paint designs on textiles that will be used for clothing, pillows, and other items. The demand for textiles with tribal designs has helped improve the economy.

The main religion in Zambia is Christianity, which was brought by European missionaries and explorers in the nineteenth century. Much like the different ethnic groups, there are many different types of Christianity practiced, from Catholicism to Lutheranism, Pentecostalism, and others. Worship

services often feature a lot of drum playing and singing.

The biggest holiday in Zambia is Christmas. Months before December 25, people begin to decorate their cities to look like African brides. The entire week between Christmas and New Year's Day is celebrated as a party.

The parties and religious celebrations continue even if the country is going through rough times. The

Drums are played during a Christian worship service. Drumming is common in many celebrations and ceremonies. Many drums are handmade.

Zambian economy relies mainly on one thing: the price of copper. Since the decline in the price of copper in the 1970s, the economy has suffered. Other governments have tried to convince Zambia's leaders to find other ways for the country to make money, such as through tourism or agriculture. However, Zambia's leaders have been slow to respond and explore other areas for the economy to grow.

fun FACTS

On the Zambian flag, red represents the struggle for freedom; black, the people of Zambia; orange, the country's mineral wealth; and green, its natural resources. The eagle in flight symbolizes freedom in Zambia and the ability to rise above the country's problems.

fun FACTS

Another reason the economy suffers is because many children cannot afford to go to school. Public schools in Zambia are free until a child reaches seventh grade. After that, many children drop out. Although the lower grades are free, there are still school fees to pay, and children are also required to wear uniforms. Many Zambians cannot afford these costs, so their children do not attend school at all. Students take classes that are very similar to those taught in the United States and Britain.

Many times, children who are lucky enough to have a uniform do not have any other clothes to

Children in schools have to share resources. Students huddle around only a few textbooks as they follow their teacher's lesson.

wear. They will stay naked on days they do not have school, because they do not want to ruin their school clothes.

Despite the poverty and the large number of children that go uneducated, nothing has hurt Zambia more than the AIDS **epidemic** (eh-pih-DEH-

Three boys read books at the First Lubuto Library in Lusaka. The Lubuto Library Project has created several libraries to serve street kids in Zambia.

mik). The disease especially affects the poor areas, where people cannot afford the medicines needed to treat AIDS. Many people are embarrassed that they have AIDS, so they do not seek treatment. Some people with AIDS are turned away from their villages. The disease kills thousands of people every year. In 2007, it was estimated that 600,000 children in Zambia lost their parents to AIDS. It is a common sight to see orphaned children sleeping under bridges or in the street.

According to the British Broadcast Corporation (BBC), AIDS has also caused the deaths of many of Zambia's professional people, including engineers and politicians. Losing these leaders has slowed Zambia's progress even more.

In 2004, the government of Zambia declared AIDS to be a national emergency. Many world aid groups have gotten involved in making Africa a priority. In 2008, U.S. President George W. Bush authorized billions of American dollars to help fight AIDS in Africa, and popular television shows such as *American Idol* have raised money to help stop the spread of AIDS there.

The effort is coming too late for many of Africa's AIDS orphans—including Franco. After losing both of his parents to the disease, he had to live for years on one meal of porridge a day at a rescue center.

Others are not as lucky as Franco. Benson Kapoma, an eighty-eight-year-old man, forages through the bush every day to try to find things he can eat. When he finds nothing, he begs. "All seven of my children died of AIDS," he said. "Now I am old and I have no one to take care of me."

Zambia

The author holds Franco, a Zambian boy who became an orphan when his parents died of AIDS.

Mulishani, *Franco!*

Chapter

When Franco walked into our classroom the next day, I was surprised to see how small he looked. He was our age but was a lot shorter and skinnier. Mr. Sagarin had told us the day before that when Franco was in Zambia, he did not have healthy foods to eat. I figured that with more food, Franco would soon be as tall and strong as the rest of us in the class.

Franco knew a lot of English words, since English is still the official language of Zambia. But he also spoke very quickly in his local language, Bemba. He taught us how to say a couple of words:

English	Bemba
Hello	mulishani (MOO-LEE-shon-ee)
Yes	eya ye (AY-yah yah)
No	awe (ah-WAY)
Thank you	twa to te la (twah TOH tee lah)
How much does it cost?	shinga (shin-GAH)
Too much!	fingi (FIN-gee)

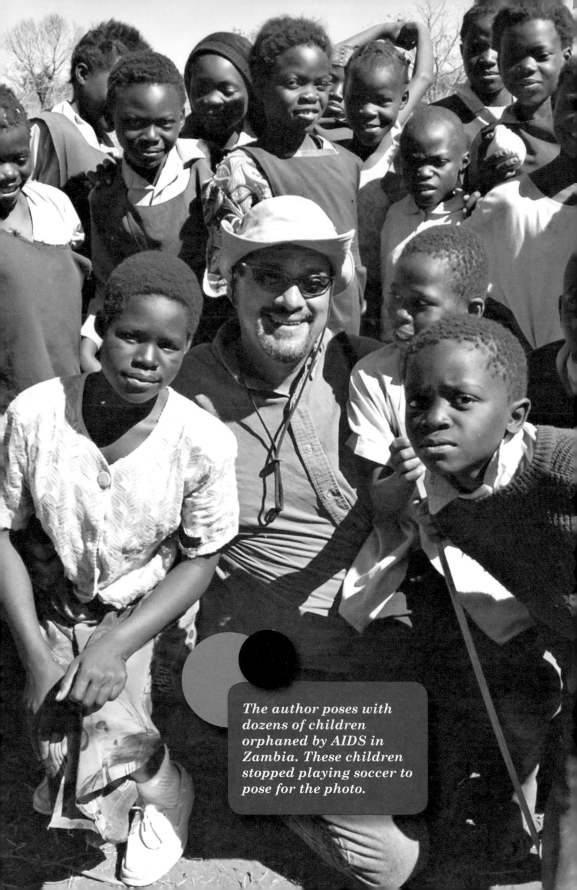

The author poses with dozens of children orphaned by AIDS in Zambia. These children stopped playing soccer to pose for the photo.

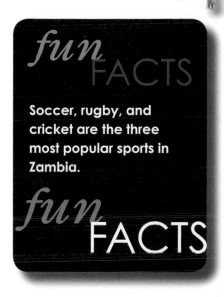

We all loved saying *mulishani* over and over, but saying *twa to te la* was a bit of a tongue twister.

Franco seemed very shy, so Mr. Sagarin joked around with him for a while until he seemed to relax. I was thrilled when he was assigned the desk right next to mine. I didn't want to seem rude, but I could not stop staring at him. Finally he looked up at me and smiled.

Just before lunch, Mr. Sagarin made another announcement. We would be eating lunch at our desks, because he had cooked up a little surprise for Franco. Mr. Sagarin made a traditional Zambian meal called **nshima** (shee-MAH). He explained that it is made from maize (corn) flour called mealie meal. It is served at almost every Zambian meal, usually with another dish made with meat or vegetables. For poor folks, though, it *is* the meal. He also made another Zambian dish, pineapple chutney, to go with it.

He put a scoop of *nshima* on a plastic plate for everyone and we tried it. Franco started smiling more when he saw that we all seemed to like it. It was thick like oatmeal but tasted a little bit like mashed potatoes. Then Mr. Sagarin mixed in some pineapple chutney. It looked like yellow relish, and gave the food a sweeter taste.

Franco told us that he liked to eat *nshima* with a special cabbage relish. He laughed when we all said, "Ewwww!"

Even though he had an accent, I was surprised at how good Franco's English was. He told me that he was lucky enough to be adopted by a family in the United States, and that he was happy to be an African and an American.

After lunch, he and I played checkers. I lost three games in a row.

"Tomorrow," he said, "maybe we can play football."

"Do you mean football or soccer?" I asked him.

He laughed and said, "Oh yes, I forgot that you call it soccer. Tomorrow we can play soccer."

I told him that my favorite player was Freddy Adu, and

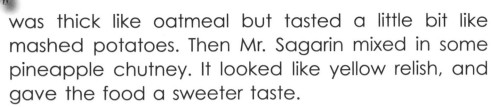

Freddy Adu

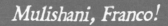

Children in Zambia play checkers. They use a wooden board with painted red squares and soda bottle caps as pieces.

he told me his favorite player is a national hero in his country. His name is Kalusha Bwalya.

Bwalya is known in Zambia as the greatest soccer player ever. He holds most of the records, including the number of goals scored. In 1996, he was **nominated** (NAH-mih-nay-ted) for the FIFA world player of the year. He went on to become the

Zambian star soccer player Kalusha Bwayla (in yellow) battles for the ball with Nigerian soccer stars. The soccer match was held to promote the FIFA 2010 World Cup hosted by South Africa.

president of the Football Association of Zambia. But what most Zambians remember about the great Kalusha Bwalya is that he scored three goals against the powerful Italian team in a 4-0 victory during the 1988 Olympics.

I had never heard of Kalusha Bwalya, but it didn't matter. I had a feeling that I would be learning a lot more about him from my new friend, Franco.

How To Make
Nshima with Pineapple Chutney

In Zambia, *nshima* is eaten at least twice a day. For those who can afford it, it is served with cooked vegetables, meat, fish, or poultry.

Chutney Ingredients

1 cup green pepper
½ cup onions
1 lb. fresh tomatoes
1 whole lemon with peel left on
1 whole orange with peel left on
1 cup fresh or canned pineapple
½ cup black raisins
1 cup white vinegar
½ cup sugar
½ cup dark brown sugar
4 Tbs. preserved candied ginger, cut in thin strips, or 1 tsp. powdered ginger
1 Tbs. salt

1. With the help of an adult, cut the first six ingredients into ½ inch cubes.
2. Mix all the ingredients in a large saucepan.
2. Have an adult turn the stove on low. Simmer gently for 30 minutes.
3. If the mixture appears thick, add 1 cup pineapple juice.
4. Serve warm or cold on crackers or with *nshima*.

Nshima Ingredients

4 cups of water
2 cups cornmeal

1. Pour 4 cups of water into a medium-sized cooking pot. With an adult's help, heat the water for 3 to 4 minutes or until lukewarm.
2. One tablespoonful at a time, slowly sprinkle ¼ cup of the cornmeal into the pot while stirring continuously. Keep stirring slowly until the mixture begins to thicken and boil.
3. Turn the heat to medium, cover the pot, and let it simmer for 3 to 5 minutes.
4. Carefully take off the lid. Slowly, a little at a time, add 1¼ cups of cornmeal. Stir briskly until the mixture is smooth and thick. Use a little more cornmeal for thicker *nshima*, or a little less for thinner *nshima*.
5. Cover, turn the heat off, and let it sit on the stove for 2 to 3 minutes. Serves 4 people.

How to Make a
Tonga Basket

You Will Need

Glue

5-inch plate

**Black and tan
construction paper**

Pencil

Scissors

Clear tape

Ruler

Basket weaving is an art form in Zambia, which claims to have the best weavers in the world. The baskets are made out of a wide variety of materials, but mainly grass reeds are used for containers. Bamboo is also a popular choice, and there are many thickets of bamboo throughout the country. When bamboo is cut down, it does not have to be replanted. The plants have a strong root system that just sprout up again.

Instructions

1 Cut 8 strips of black construction paper and 8 strips of tan construction paper about 12 inches long and ¾ inch wide.

2 Glue the ends of the 12-inch-long pieces together, letting them overlap a little bit.

3 When the glue is dry, cut 4 strips 16 inches long out of what's been glued. Glue these strips together at the middle, fanning them out to form a star. These strips will be the frame of your basket.

4 Using a 5-inch plate as a guide, draw a circle on another piece of construction paper. Cut out the circle and glue it to the center of the star. This circle will be the bottom of your basket. (If you want, you can use a 5-inch square at the bottom instead.)

5 Fold the edges of the star up from the bottom. Tape the rest of the long strip to one of the strips coming up from the star, near the bottom. Weave this new strip over and under the rays of the star all the way around.

6 When that strip has been woven through, take the tape off and glue the ends of the strip to the basket. You may need to hold the paper together until the glue begins to dry.

7 Fold the ends of the frame over the woven strip and into the basket. Glue them in place. This will form a rim.

Further Reading

Books

Bryan, Ashley. *The Night Has Ears: African Proverbs*. New York: Atheneum, 1999.

Krensky, Stephen, and Jeni Reeves. *The Lion and the Hare: An East African Folktale*. Minneapolis, MN: Millbrook Press, 2009.

Oguneye, Kunle, and Bruce McCorkindale. *Sikulu and Harambe by the Zambezi River: An African Version of the Good Samaritan Story*. Renton, WA: Blue Brush Media, 2008.

Works Consulted

This story is based on the author's personal trip to Zambia in 2006, and on an interview with Benson Kapoma in Zambia, 2006. Other sources he used are listed below.

Else, David. *Lonely Planet: Zambia*. Victoria, Australia: Lonely Planet Publications, 2002.

McIntyre, Chris. *Bradt Travel Guide: Zambia*. Guilford, CT: Globe Pequot Press, 2008.

Musambachime, Mwelwa. *Basic Facts on Zambia*. Bloomington, IN: AuthorHouse, 2005.

Taylor, Scott. *Culture and Customs of Zambia*. Santa Barbara, CA: Greenwood Press, 2006.

Waters, Bella. *Zambia in Pictures*. Breckenridge, CO: Twenty-First Century Books, 2009.

On the Internet

All Africa: Zambia
http://allafrica.com/zambia/

BBC News Country Profile: Zambia
http://news.bbc.co.uk/2/hi/africa/country_profiles/1069294.stm

Central Intelligence Agency: The World Factbook: Zambia
https://www.cia.gov/library/publications/the-world-factbook/geos/za.html

Football Association of Zambia
http://www.fazfootball.com

Global Health Reporting: Zambia
http://www.globalhealthreporting.org/article.asp?DR_ID=57286

Further Reading

Lubuto Library Project
   http://www.lubuto.org
U.S. Department of State: Zambia
   http://www.state.gov/r/pa/ei/bgn/2359.htm

Embassy
The Embassy of the Republic of Zambia
2419 Massachusetts Avenue, NW
Washington, DC 20008
Telephone: (202) 265-9717
Fax: (202) 332-0826
http://www.zambiaembassy.org/
Email: embzambia@aol.com

Zambian kwacha—front (left); back (below)

20 ngwee

1 kwacha

PHOTO CREDITS: Cover—Ian Murphy/Getty Images; p. 1—JupiterImages; pp. 2–3, 4, 5, 8, 10, 18, 21, 23, 24, 26, 27, 28, 29, 31, 32; p. 11—courtesy of Michael Mistretta; p. 12—Hulton Archive/Getty Images; p. 16—Per Arne Wilson/GFDL/cc-by-sa-3.0; p. 17—UN Photo; p. 20—Mehmet Karatay/cc-by-sa-3.0; pp. 34, 35, 36, 39, 43—courtesy of John Torres; p. 40—Pius Utomi Ekpei/AFP/Getty Images. Every effort has been made to locate all copyright holders of material used in this book. If any errors or omissions have occurred, corrections will be made in future editions of the book.

Glossary

AIDS—A deadly disease that strikes a person's immune system. This disease continues to kill millions of people in Africa each year.

charities (CHAYR-ih-teez)—Organizations or institutions designed to help those in need.

colonize (KAH-luh-nyz)—To migrate to an area and occupy it as a group.

epidemic (eh-pih-DEH-mik)—A disease that spreads quickly throughout an area, affecting many people.

malaria (mah-LAYR-ee-uh)—A deadly disease spread by mosquitoes that causes a high fever and sometimes death.

missionary (MIH-shuh-nayr-ee)—Someone who travels in order to help others and to spread the religion of Christianity.

nominate (NAH-mih-nayt)—To name someone for an award, office, or position.

nshima (shee-MAH)—The most popular meal of Zambia, made primarily of cornmeal and water.

poverty (PAH-ver-tee)—The condition of having or making less money than it takes to live a normal life.

primitive (PRIH-mih-tiv)—Living simply; not very advanced in areas of science such as technology or medicine.

slave traders—People who went to Africa to capture people and sell them as slaves.

subsistence (sub-SIS-tents)—The means by which one survives or maintains life; the minimum amount needed for survival.

Index

Adu, Freddy   38
AIDS   9, 11, 17, 31–33, 34, 36
Angola   7, 13
Banda, Rupiah Bwezani   17
Bangweulu Swamps   19, 20
Bantu   13
Barefoot Wilderness Camp
    24
Botswana   7, 13
Bush, George W.   33
Bwalya, Kalusha   39–40
child care   10
Congo, Democratic
    Republic of the   6, 13
Congo basin   19
copper   6, 16, 30
Hudson Valley, New York   5
Lacerda, Francisco de   14
Liberia   8
Livingstone, David   12, 14–
    15, 19
Luangwa River Valley   19, 24
Lubuto Library Project   32
Lusaka   4, 6, 25, 32
malaria   22–23
Malawi   6, 13
Mosi-oa-Tunya   (see Victoria
    Falls)
Mozambique   6, 13
Namibia   6, 13
Ngoni   14

Nigeria   8
nshima   37
Nsokolo   14
photography   11
Rhodes, Cecil   15–16
Stanley, Henry   12
Tanzania   6, 13
textiles   28
Tonga   13
tourism   22
Victoria Falls   15, 18
Zambezi River   18, 19
Zambia
    climate of   20, 22–23
    clothing in   5, 7, 9
    family life in   25–26
    farming in   26, 27
    flag of   30
    games in   9, 38, 39
    government of   16–17, 33
    history of   12, 13–17
    languages in   6, 9
    map of   6
    music in   25. 29
    plumbing in   8, 10
    religions in   6, 25, 28
    schools in   30–31
    sports in   9, 36, 37, 38–39
    wildlife in   19–20, 21
Zimbabwe   6, 13, 18
Zulu   9

ABOUT THE AUTHOR

John A. Torres is an award-winning newspaper reporter from Central Florida. His stories have taken him to Zambia, Italy, Indonesia, Mexico, India, and Haiti. In 2006 he traveled to the African country of Zambia to report on the number of children there who have been orphaned by AIDS. In Zambia, he met a little boy named Franco, who is the inspiration for the main character in this book. Torres says, "Franco did not speak much English, but he loved to have his photograph taken. He also loved to be held. This book is dedicated to Franco, who would not leave my side for the short time that I knew him. I hope and pray that he is still alive."

A real person also inspired the teacher in this book. Torres relates, "Mr. Fred Sagarin was my second-grade teacher at Pablo Casals School in the Bronx, New York. He let us call him Fred, and he took us all to his farm on the weekends."

Torres is the author of more than 40 children's books, including *Meet Our New Student from Haiti* and *Meet Our New Student from Nicaragua* for Mitchell Lane Publishers.